The Santa Fe Trail

Ryan P. Randolph

The Rosen Publishing Group's
PowerKids Press™
New York

To my wife, Joanne, thank you for everything

Published in 2003 by The Rosen Publishing Group, Inc.
29 East 21st Street, New York, NY 10010

First Edition

Managing Editor: Kathy Kuhtz Campbell
Book Designer: Emily Muschinske

Photo Credits: Cover, title page, pp. 6, 10, 11, 14 (left), 17, 21 (inset) © North Wind Picture Archives; back cover, p. 5 © Gregory Franzwa; pp. 5 (top left), 9 (inset), 14 (right) © Nancy Carter/North Wind Picture Archives; pp. 13 (inset), 18 (inset), 21 © Getty Images; p. 13 © David Muench/CORBIS; p. 17 (inset) © The Kansas State Historical Society; p. 18 courtesy of Milstein Division of United States History, Local History & Genealogy, The New York Public Library, Astor, Lenox and Tilden Foundations.

Manufactured in the United States of America

Contents

An Age-Old Trail

Inset: *The end of the trail is marked by this 1910 monument in Santa Fe Plaza. Today the National Park Service oversees the Santa Fe National Historic Trail.*

The Santa Fe Trail began as the age-old **routes** that Native Americans used for hunting and trading. In the 1600s, Native Americans led early Spanish explorers, such as Francisco Vásquez de Coronado, along many of these trails. French traders journeyed to Santa Fe from the French colonies in America in the 1700s.

Until 1821, Mexico was a colony of Spain's. Santa Fe was the capital of northern Mexico, known today as New Mexico. Santa Fe was the closest official Spanish **outpost** to the United States and drew many American traders. American traders in Santa Fe, though, had their goods taken and were put in jail by the Spanish government. The Spanish government tried to control trade. It did not want American traders to buy and to sell the goods that Spain believed should be coming from Mexico City.

This map of the Santa Fe Trail shows the trade route that started from Independence, Missouri, and that ended at Santa Fe, New Mexico. The Mountain Route and the Cimarron Cutoff separate at Cimarron and meet again at Fort Union in the Sangre de Cristo Mountains.

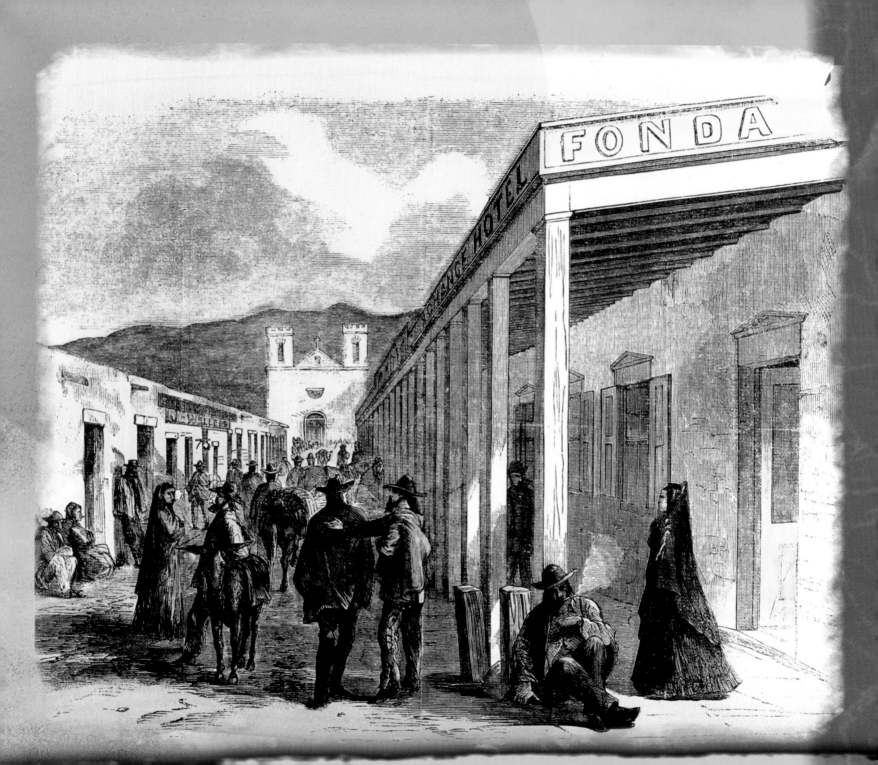

The Santa Fe Trail Opens to Trade

In 1821, Mexico gained its **independence** from Spain. The country of Mexico welcomed traders from the United States to Santa Fe. Missouri merchant William Becknell, known as the Father of the Santa Fe Trail, is believed by most people today to have made the first trip for **commerce** on the Santa Fe Trail in September 1821. Becknell found the new Mexican government very willing to trade because American goods, such as tools and other important supplies, were not available in Mexico. Becknell sold these goods in Santa Fe for a huge **profit**. He was said to return to Franklin, Missouri, with gold and silver in his saddlebags.

An 1860s woodcut shows busy San Francisco Street in Santa Fe. After Mexico won its independence from Spain in 1821, Santa Fe became an important trading town for American and Mexican merchants.

DID YOU KNOW?

On their second trip to Santa Fe, Becknell and his men almost died of thirst. They took the Cimarron Cutoff across the desert where there was no water. To stay alive, they killed a buffalo to drink water from its stomach.

The Mountain Route

The Santa Fe Trail had different starting points in Missouri and in Kansas. Most travelers favored two major paths across the **prairies**, the rivers, and the mountains west of Council Grove, Kansas. After a flood destroyed the town of Franklin, Missouri, in 1828, people used Independence, Missouri, as their starting point. Other traders left from Westport Landing, which today is known as Kansas City, Missouri.

When Becknell and his four companions made their first trip to Santa Fe, they began in Franklin, Missouri. They traveled along the Mountain Route. This path followed the Arkansas River into Colorado and ran southwest through the high, unsafe Raton Pass, before heading south to Santa Fe. Becknell's group led pack mules through Raton Pass. It would be a more difficult trip for the large wagons that would later be used on the rough trail.

Mule-drawn wagons had a hard time crossing the rocky paths of the Sangre de Cristo Mountains. Inset: A marker in Cimarron, New Mexico, tells about Becknell's opening of the Santa Fe Trail.

OFFICIAL SCENIC HISTORIC MARKER

SANTA FE TRAIL

Opened by William Becknell in 1821, the Santa Fe Trail became the major trade route to Santa Fe from Missouri River towns. The two main branches, the Cimarron Cutoff and the Mountain Branch, joined at Watrous. Travel over the Trail ceased with the coming of the railroad in 1879.

The Cimarron Cutoff

In 1822, Becknell took three wagons across the Jornada Route, or the Cimarron Cutoff. This desert route left the Arkansas River and passed Wagon Bed Spring, Rabbit Ears, and Round Mound. The Mountain Route and the Cimarron Cutoff met at Fort Union, on the southern edge of the Sangre de Cristo Mountains. From there the trail led to Santa Fe.

Using the Cimarron Cutoff shortened the trip to Santa Fe by 100 miles (161 km) and by 10 days. The route avoided the Raton Pass. Many people used the cutoff even though there were fewer places to find food and shelter than there were along the Mountain Route.

Above: Travelers on the Cimarron Cutoff might have seen a female mule deer and her fawns in a dried-out riverbed. Left: The wagon-wheel ruts along the trail can be seen near Cimarron, Kansas.

DID YOU KNOW?

The Santa Fe Trail was not like today's modern highway. The 1,203-mile (1,936-km) trip from Franklin to Santa Fe took about 72 days for a wagon to travel. It took about 62 days to travel the Cimarron Cutoff to reach Santa Fe.

Covered Wagons

Beginning in 1824, traders made the trip to Santa Fe in wagon trains, or large groups of covered wagons pulled by mules or oxen. The wagons most often used were the **Conestoga wagons**. The Conestoga wagon was very big and could carry about 6 tons (5.4 t) of cargo. It had a bottom that curved up at each end to keep the wagon's contents from falling out. Canvas, or a white, heavy cloth, was held up by horseshoe-shaped arches and covered the wagon.

Teams of eight mules or oxen were used to pull each wagon. Oxen were better at pulling heavy loads and did not have to stop to rest as often as did the mules. Mules were more sure-footed than oxen and could make the trip over the rough land. Mules were often stubborn and were scared easily, which made travel more difficult.

The Conestoga wagon (a modern copy is seen here) was named for an area in Pennsylvania known as Conestoga Creek, where Dutch settlers built the first Conestoga wagons in the early 1700s. Inset: Usually oxen were used to pull the covered wagons along the Santa Fe Trail.

Fort Union

Sangre de Cristo Mountains

From Bugs to Blizzards

The trip to Santa Fe was not easy. Travelers usually began in the spring to avoid cold weather. It was often very hot and dusty. Sometimes wagon trains **encountered** flooding streams, raging storms, and even spring blizzards. Bugs, such as mosquitoes and gnats, pestered the travelers. Travelers often saw rattlesnakes on the sandy hills along the banks of the Arkansas River. Buffalo, elk, antelope, and prairie dogs were also seen along the trail. When travelers spotted a buffalo, they often hunted it as a source of meat. Most of the trip to Santa Fe passed through flat prairies. Travelers could spend some uneventful days without seeing animals or other people.

On the trail, travelers passed many sights, including the beautiful Sangre de Cristo Mountains and Fort Union, a military fort that guarded the trail.

DID YOU KNOW?

Lieutenant Colonel Ewin Sumner built Fort Union in 1851 to help protect the Santa Fe Trail. For the next 40 years, three different forts occupied the area. Today the National Park Service protects the ruins of the fort.

15

Life on the Santa Fe Trail

When traders formed a wagon train, they first had to choose a captain or a leader. Then each person in the train was given a job to do during the journey. Everyone helped to do chores, such as collecting wood or buffalo **manure**, called chips, for fuel, hunting for food, or standing guard at night.

On the trail, crews woke up at dawn and **hitched** the animals to the wagons. The wagon train headed on the trail with great noise and cries of "All set!" and "Catch up! Catch up!" Travel was stopped before noon to rest and to graze the oxen or the mules and to eat the main meal of the day. This meal might include salt pork, bread, beans, and coffee.

Wagon trains continued down the trail into the afternoon. The camp for the night was set up before sunset.

Travelers along the Santa Fe Trail set up camps every evening. They cared for their animals, made repairs to the wagons, chose that night's guards, and then slept for a few hours. Inset: Fur trapper and explorer Jedediah Smith traveled along the Santa Fe Trail. While searching for water on the trail in 1831, Smith was killed by some Native Americans called the Comanche.

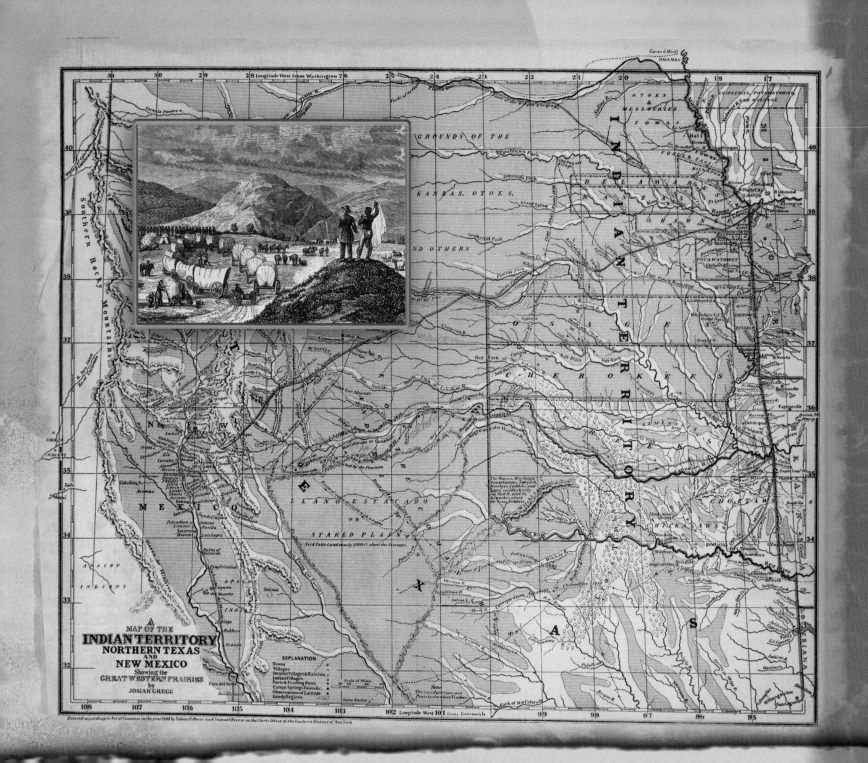

A
MAP OF THE
INDIAN TERRITORY
NORTHERN TEXAS
AND
NEW MEXICO
Showing the
GREAT WESTERN PRAIRIES
by
JOSIAH GREGG

EXPLANATION

Towns
Villages
Smaller Villages & Ranchos
Indian Villages
Forts & Trading Posts
Camps Springs Ruins &c.
Observations of Latitude
Sandy Regions

Scale of Miles

Note:
The tinted portions are
Prairie, the white Timber.

Entered according to Act of Congress in the year 1844 by Sidney E. Morse and Samuel Breese in the Clerks Office of the Southern District of New York.

Entering Native American Homelands

The Santa Fe Trail crossed the homelands and hunting grounds of several Native American peoples, including the Pawnee, the Comanche, the Kiowa, the Osage, the Kansas, and the Pueblos. **Tensions** grew between Native Americans and white traders. The incoming travelers forced Native Americans from their lands. Attacks by Native Americans became more frequent as the unwanted traffic along the trails increased.

The travelers protected themselves by steering the wagons in two or four columns so they could be moved easily into a circle to shield them from attacks. Sometimes the U.S. Army provided armed **escorts** for the wagons.

This map of the southern plains appeared in a book written by trader Josiah Gregg, who made about 12 trips on the Santa Fe Trail. It was the most dependable map of the area in the 1840s. Inset: Camp Comanche was a trading camp on the Santa Fe Trail.

DID YOU KNOW?

Susan Shelby Magoffin kept a diary of her 1846 trip on the Santa Fe Trail and was considered to be the first woman to make the trip. In truth, Mary Dodson Donoho was the first. She left Council Grove, Kansas, for Santa Fe in 1833.

The Army Protects the Trail

Trading companies built the first **forts** along the Santa Fe Trail. The major fort along the trail was Bent's Fort, which brothers Charles and William Bent and their partner Ceran de St. Vrain built in 1833. As did many forts along the trail, it provided a safe place to rest and to buy supplies.

In the 1830s, the U.S. Army began to use the trail to **transport** military supplies. The army built forts as tensions between the United States and Mexico increased. In 1846, the Mexican War began. That year, U.S. general Stephen W. Kearny led the Army of the West down the trail and took Santa Fe from Mexico without firing a shot. In 1848, the United States and Mexico signed an agreement called the Treaty of Guadalupe Hidalgo. This treaty ended the war and made New Mexico a U.S. **territory**. Santa Fe was named the territorial capital in 1851.

Inset: *On August 18, 1846, General Stephen W. Kearny captured Santa Fe without a fight.* Right: *On September 14, 1847, U.S. general Winfield Scott led troops into Mexico City, ending the war.*

The Railroads Take Over

The use of railroads across the Great Plains in the 1860s caused trade along the Santa Fe Trail to **decline**, or to go down. Railroads could carry goods cheaper and quicker than could wagon trains. In 1880, workers hired by the Atchison, Topeka, and Santa Fe Railroad Company finally finished laying the tracks to Santa Fe. The days of the wagon trains rolling along the trail were finished.

In 1987, U.S. president Ronald Reagan signed a law creating the Santa Fe National Historic Trail. The National Park Service works with other groups to protect the trail and the buildings and sites along it.

Today the ruts, or tracks, left in the ground by the wheels of the heavy wagons can still be seen along the Santa Fe Trail. The trail's story continues to be told for all who wish to enjoy it.

Glossary

commerce (KAH-mers) Buying or selling items on a large scale, which involves shipping goods from place to place.

Conestoga wagons (kah-nuh-STOH-guh WA-gins) A type of four-wheeled vehicle pulled by large animals that was used to travel across prairies.

decline (dih-KLYN) To get weaker or to approach the end of something.

encountered (en-KOWN-terd) To have met by chance.

escorts (ES-korts) People who go along with others to protect them.

forts (FORTS) Strong buildings that can be defended against enemy attack.

hitched (HICHT) To have attached animals to a wagon or another object.

independence (in-dih-PEN-dents) Freedom from the rule, the control, the support, or the help of other people.

manure (muh-NOOR) Waste matter from animals that is used to fertilize soil. When it is dried, it can be used as fuel.

outpost (OWT-pohst) A settlement, a small fort, or a place that is far away from other places.

prairies (PRAYR-eez) Large, grassy lands that can be flat or rolling.

profit (PRAH-fit) The money a person or a company makes after all the bills or the costs are paid.

routes (ROOTS) Established paths used to travel between places.

tensions (TEN-shunz) The pressure or the strain between two groups of people or things.

territory (TEHR-uh-tohr-ee) Land that is controlled by a person or a group of people.

transport (trans-PORT) To move something from one place to another.

Index

Web Sites

To learn more about the Santa Fe Trail, check out these Web sites:

www.larned.net/trailctr/
www.nmhu.edu/research/sftrail/default.htm

Primary Sources

Page 6. *San Francisco Street, Santa Fe, New Mexico.* A colored woodcut from the 1860s shows the bustling plaza in Santa Fe and the adobe church La Parroquia, which had stood since 1714 at the end of the street. The Romanesque Cathedral of St. Francis, begun in 1869, later replaced the adobe church. **Page 9.** *On the Way to New Diggings—Halt in a Rough Pass of the Rocky Mountains.* This wood engraving appeared in *Harper's Weekly* on May 1, 1875. *Harper's Weekly* was a major illustrated magazine in the United States. It began publication in 1857. The original illustration was printed in black and white in the magazine and was hand colored sometime after 1875. **Page 17 (inset).** *Portrait of Jedediah Smith.* This picture of the mountain man Jedediah Smith is a copy of a painting that was done between 1823 and 1831. **Page 18 (inset).** *Camp Comanche.* This 1839 engraving was published in Josiah Gregg's book *Commerce of the Prairies.* Gregg's book contained his travel notes about the Santa Fe Trail and was published in two volumes in 1844. The engraving of Camp Comanche appears on page 36 of Volume 2. The engraving shows the trading camp on the Santa Fe Trail, between the North Fork and the Canadian River, in what was called Indian Territory. Soldiers guard the camp, which includes a wagon train that has been formed in a circle for protection against attacks by unfriendly Native Americans. Gregg's book became a best-seller, appeared in at least six editions, sold well in England, and was translated into French and German. Many historians believe it is still one of the most important stories for the study of the Santa Fe Trail today. **Page 18.** *Map of the Indian Territory, Northern Texas, and New Mexico, Showing the Great Western Prairies.* In 1845, Josiah Gregg produced the most reliable map of the southern plains of that period. The map printed here was published by Lakeside Press in a 1926 reprint of *Commerce of the Prairies.*